If Only Today

Inspirational messages for everyday
of the year

∞

Shontel Stanford

Copyright © 2009 by Shontel Stanford.

ISBN: Softcover   978-1-4415-1881-1

All rights reserved. No part of this book may be reproduced or transmitted in any form or by any means, electronic or mechanical, including photocopying, recording, or by any information storage and retrieval system, without permission in writing from the copyright owner.

This book was printed in the United States of America.

To order additional copies of this book, contact:
Xlibris Corporation
1-888-795-4274
www.Xlibris.com
Orders@Xlibris.com

Mesh,

To you, beautiful woman of God, be led by the Spirit of God and watch you blossom like the rose you are.

Love,

ID

I pray that you be encouraged in heart and that your faith will increase in Him. As you run this race of life you must not get weary because you know if you finish you will be rewarded greatly by Jesus Christ, our Savior. Do not focus on the trials of the world but keep your eyes on the Lord, our God, and He will satisfy you. We are more than conquerors, a peculiar people, set apart to God; we are His righteousness and should act as such. As you live according to His holy word He will manifest Himself through you. Shield your heart from the cares of this world and renew your mind daily in Christ. Let this word minister to your spirit and encourage someone else. Thank the Lord in all things and walk in the blessing! In Jesus' name, Amen.

1 Just when you think you have reached the end and you can't go any further God will give you the strength to keep going. Keep moving . . .

2 Love, forgive again and again, strive to never give up or give in, listen and obey God, read the word, speak the word and live the word but most important love God and love with the love of God to conquer all.

3 Be thankful, stay humble, live grateful! By the blood of Jesus you have been set free!

4 Lord, I know nothing is possible without You. Please help me to always remember that I could do nothing on my own because without You I am lost and all alone.

5 We can never know how much Jesus really loves us to have sacrificed His precious life for the sins of you and me. Just meditate on that sight and pray that God would teach us to love everyone that much.

6 You are going to make it! No matter what it looks like, no matter what the enemy says, no matter how it may feel. God hasn't brought you this far to let you go now. Be encourage . . . you're going to make it.

7 If it wasn't for God you wouldn't be alive, if it wasn't for Jesus you wouldn't have gotten another chance, and if it wasn't for the devil's attacks you would never know what it feels like to overcome.

8 Saturate God with your praise not your complaints. When you begin to praise Him you forget what you were complaining about in the first place.

9 God is only limited by what you give to Him. If you continue to carry your own problems and try to provide your own blessings you limit Him from being your God.

10 When you hear the word continue to speak it until you see what you have been speaking come to pass.

11 Lord, I declare this day that I am the righteousness of God. I declare the bread of Heaven is raining into my life and every area of my life is full of God's goodness right now.

12 Greater is He that is in you. When you allow Him to rule in your heart then you will not be defeated no matter what the enemy throws your way. You have to know that you win.

13 When God shows you what way to go Satan will come with an alternative route that looks better, but know God caters to spirit while Satan caters to flesh.

14 When the enemy tells you that you are weak rejoice that the Lord is your strength because in the area of your weakness is where God can show Himself strong if you allow Him.

15 It is possible to be doing the will of God and going the wrong way. That is why God puts us under a covering of a church and spiritual leaders that can help us to stay straight because they have already been where you are.

16 When God tells you to speak don't withhold the word because it may be what someone else needs to hear to keep walking with God.

17 You have to see what God sees in you but if you never make any moves towards your destiny it will pass you by. Prepare yourself and begin to walk in your calling.

18 Stop saying you can't, God knows how much you can handle because He created you and no more will be put on you than you can bear so that means YOU CAN but you have to speak it.

19 Satan may use people to hurt you but remember God loves everyone and you must still treat them the way you would treat God.

20 A lot of people will say they are following God but it is only to get close to you so hide yourself in the Word so that you will hear God and know who is really of Him.

21 Don't expect more from another person than you would expect from yourself because only Jesus was born to carry the burdens of the world.

22 You cannot be broken or destroyed when you are in Jesus because He is your protector. Satan may come but He has to get through Jesus to get to you so do not be afraid of anything.

23 When you have a need that is not the time to be quiet but you should cry out to God until you have gotten His attention and what you came for.

24 To be like Christ is to be a servant, to give all that you have. We are naturally born selfish people but the more that we give of ourselves the more that we will die to our selfishness.

25 Allow God to be your companion instead of continuing to look for one because you will keep setting yourself up for failure. When the time is right God will send your mate.

26 Don't dwell on your mistakes because Jesus came to restore you, just lean on Him as He walks with you.

27 Children look up to their parents and can't wait until they grow up to be like them . . . if we could only keep that mentality toward our heavenly Father.

28 Isn't it good to know that God knows all before you even say anything and He will send what you need if you ask, when you least expect it.

29 Don't allow anything to come in that will dilute your faith because weak faith cannot be effective to do the will of God.

30 We, as humans, try to block tribulation from coming to us but we neglect to realize God allows these things to come in to make us stronger.

31 Every time the enemy comes with a storm remember what God has already done for you and rest on that, knowing He will do it again.

32 If you come into His presence, God will never send you away empty handed.

33 Soak up the Word so no matter how life squeezes you the Word will continue to come out.

34 As you grow make sure that it is in Christ and not in yourself. Get back to the basics and never forget where you came from and what you came for.

35 You can't decide to believe God after you get your miracle because it's going to take you believing before you receive to reach out for your miracle.

36 If Jesus tells you to "Come" you can't afford to be afraid because that will block your faith.

37 When God mends something it doesn't come apart ever again.

38 God, I need you to help me. I seem to keep making the same mistakes and I feel like I'm failing you. I come again to be forgiven and made new. Show me Your word that I may know how to live holy unto You.

39 This walk is not to be done alone. You have to surround yourself with the Word and strong believers that will help you along.

40 It doesn't matter what someone else believes about your situation, but it's about what you believe that God looks at to determine your faith in Him.

41 When God tells you to do something, it is to bring you closer to Him not to take you further away so make sure you follow the Word.

42 If the devil is not attacking you then something is wrong because when you are following God the devil will always TRY to distract you but you will always overcome through Christ.

43 When it comes to doing wrong you can do it so well but when it comes to doing good it seems that you just can't get the hang of it but don't be discourage, Jesus will continue to work with you and you'll get it right if you dwell in Him.

44 When you yield your life to God you are going to have to let some things and some people go to reach Him. Satan will use those things to keep pulling you back into your old ways when God wants to give you something new.

45 God, I pray that you know my heart and that it is pure towards You. I want so much just to do Your will and I ask that You lead me through it.

46 I'm not like anyone else because He made me unique. I have my own talents, dreams and goals. He created me for a purpose that can only be fulfilled by me. Despite how I may have gotten here I am HERE!

47 Realize there is no place you can hide from Him. Just as He knows your thoughts He knows where you are at all times. You can try to run and hide from Him but He will always find you. Your spirit is connected to Him so you can never hide.

48 God knows you better than anyone, even better than yourself. There's not a thought or desire you have that He doesn't know. It's amazing that someone so great knows you so well and He still loves you.

49 God wants you to have more of Him so when trials come you know how to deal with them. You must study everyday not just Sunday. You can't play the game if you don't train.

50 You are what you say you are . . . you have what you believe you have . . . if you believe God what isn't possible for you is possible through Him if you believe.

51 God is amazing in all His ways. He will send you into the place of your blessing and position you to stand if you will listen, hear and obey what He is saying.

52 When you're obeying God you don't have to look for your blessing because it will find you. Nothing will stop your blessing but you just have to line up with Him.

53 If you really want to get right with God you have to start now because you can't expect a change if you don't reposition yourself. Change starts in YOU. Don't say "you know, you're trying or you want to" anymore . . . just do it.

54 The flesh will never want to do what God wants you to (go to church, praise God, pay your tithes and give an offering, or live right) but to follow God you have to deny your flesh.

55 There is no need to be ashamed when you know that God has forgiven you. Let it go and move on because Satan will keep throwing it in your face if you let him.

56 Make sure it's what God wants and not just you. A lot of times we do things that FEEL right to us and not God's will.

57 You have to be willing to change no matter who is around because Satan knows what tempts you and he is going to try to trip you up no matter where you go.

58 You can't imagine the ways God wants to bless you if you line up with His will. Many times you miss your blessing because you tell Him to have His way while you continue to do your own thing.

59 How can you wake up every morning and go to sleep every night without spending time with God, who keeps you safe all day? He is there but you still need to invite Him in.

60 You're blessed. It may not be the blessing you were looking for but God said it's the one you need so rejoice because when you're not looking is when your true blessing comes.

61 All God ask is that He be lifted up and He will do the rest so give Him the praise and watch everything fall in place.

62 Don't be that one that puts a stumbling block in front of your brother, we are to lift one another up and by building others we will build ourselves up.

63 God commands you to be forgiving of those who hurt you if you want to be forgiven by God. Yes, it may hurt but how can you ever move on if you hold on to what they did?

64 It's not that you ever deserved the second chance that you have been granted but that God loved you enough to credit it to you on His Son's behalf.

65 You get mad about not receiving what you want but neglect to thank God for your basic needs, which He supplies. How does that look?

66 Make sure that when you hear the word you let it marinate in your soul because satan is going to come suddenly to give you a pop quiz and you have to use what you learned to pass.

67 People are going to talk about you no matter what you say or do so keep your eyes on the goal and know that nothing can separate you from the love of God.

68 What you see in someone else, someone else will see in you so be careful that you see what God sees and not man.

69 It's a choice, you have to choose to live for God, not yourself, it is then your life will turn around.

70 In God there is always a process and a season for everything so in this season trust God. For even the Earth knows if we never went through Fall what would blossom in Spring?

71 You are where you are today because of what you have thought and spoke but once your thinking is lined up with Gods' thinking you will see the manifestation of His power in you.

72 When you are faced with a problem don't talk to all of your friends about it instead take it to the only One who can solve the issue. Jesus.

73 Don't ask God to bless you if you are not ready to except the blessing.

74 Other people may do things that you know is not of God but you must hate the sin, not the person.

75 You say you want to be like Christ but you don't want to suffer like Him, you only want the reward, but if you make no sacrifice where is room for gain.

76 God wants the real you. Not the superficial façade you put on in front of your friends, He wants the broken person that needs to be put back together.

77 We know when we are sinning but the hard part is admitting that we slipped. The joy is that God already knew that's why He sent Jesus so we could repent and get back on track.

78 No matter how hard you try to fight it, you are broken when you come face to face with God. You see your dirt but He will make you clean. That is where you start.

79 Your plans are not always God's plan but if your plan gets in His way He will reassign you.

80 God is full of humor, such an amazing character. If you listen close you'll hear Him laugh just as we do at our silly mistakes.

81 We never see how dirty we are when we are in a mud bath, it's not until we come out that we see how far we have sunk.

82 He said bring your tithes into the storehouse and TRY ME. He promised if you sow the seed you will reap the harvest. Give your tithe and offering to Him first and He will supply more for you.

83 God is still God before your trials, during your trials and after your trials. He is faithful to HIS CHILDREN but you can't only call Him when things are going wrong . . .

84 God wants to free you but it requires a change on your part. You can't be freed if you're going to turn around and do the same thing.

85 If you want God you have to obey despite how you feel because your flesh will never want to be in God's presence but that is where your healing is. That is where your breakthrough is. That is where your new beginning is.

86 Faith comes by HEARING but so does everything else . . . after you continue to hear the same things you speak them into your life so listen to God and what is good.

87 The Word says the spirit is willing but the flesh is weak. You can't allow your weak flesh to overpower your willing spirit and just excuse it as no big deal. God has called us to holiness so build your spirit man up.

88 What good is it to have the knowledge of the Word but never put it to use in your life?

89 We are like a vase with a crack, imperfect, but the Holy Spirit is the water that fills us and if allowed to keep pouring when we break nothing but the Spirit will flow out.

90 You are royalty but if you don't know it no one will treat you as such. God has made you an heir so walk in your royalty.

91 You need to believe that God can do it and then walk into it by the work He has for you to do and you will see it come to pass.

92 YOU CAN WIN! Jesus said the way is difficult but it is not impossible.

93 The rock of your salvation is Jesus Christ. He does not sway like water but He is firmly set so that you may build on Him and not be moved.

94 God moves when you honor Him.

95 There may be things in your life that hinder you from God's call but you are afraid of losing them so they become more important than God . . . do you not see you are blocking your own destiny?

96 How can you pray for someone else when you are filled with anger towards them? First pray for your forgiveness and that you forgive them.

97 Don't seek after God because you want materials things, seek Him for Him and He will bless you with those things because He will know your heart is pure.

98 When you ask God for something know that the devil will ALWAYS bring some things to make you believe you'll never have it but when God says yes no one can make it no.

99 You cannot be a teacher until you are first a student and even then you will never know everything so allow God to be your guide.

100 God has given you good gifts but being in the world has also given you bad characteristics so you need to renew your mind so that you can do those great things that you have been called for.

101 As soon as you make an attempt to do the will of God (act of obedience) Satan will come to tempt you but keep your mind set on God and you will prevail.

102 God has given His spirit so that in times of need we can be ministered to and restored.

103 You can't change what you did in your past but God will take who you are and make you great for His glory.

104 Don't get tired yet . . . you are someone else's hope.

105 God wants you humble and mature to receive your blessing, it is not by your word but by your actions.

106 You don't have to search for love in other people when you know that the best (God) is loving you, you just need to love yourself.

107 Don't turn away from anyone who is in need because one day you may need and who will be there for you?

108 Every thought God has for me is good. If all His thoughts are good then I should always think good of myself.

109 This walk is not easy, yes you will have haters, but you can overcome them as Christ did.

110 God will give you the opportunity to bless others but don't boast in the fact that you are able to bless because it was not yours to give, but the Lords.

111 Come to God with an open heart, He already knows what you need, but a door cannot be opened to those who don't knock.

112 A child never forgets the pain linked from their childhood but God can heal all the pain and take away the painful memories if you are willing.

113 Why do you worry and complain about things you cannot change? If you say you give it to God then leave it with Him, it is no longer your concern.

114 It seems as if people become more righteous and judgmental of others the longer they have been saved but remember when you first came to Jesus and keep that heart.

115 Be strong yet gentle. You can speak with authority without yelling to get your point across.

116 Don't declare 'if God wanted you to have something He would give it to you' if you have put forth no effort it will not happen.

117 People hurt over material losses because they put so much value into them but if your heart and mind are on Christ all will be restored.

118 NO one can fill that void in you except God so no matter who you run to you will always leave the same until you go to your Creator.

119 You cannot fight someone else's battle. That is between them and God. It is for you to be their moral support and pray that God will see them through.

120 Even if no one else wanted you God did. God picked us even though we weren't deserving to make us heirs to the throne.

121 Ask yourself, "Am I dying enough?" We know that the only way to get closer to God is that our flesh has to die so are you laying on the Altar everyday?

122 Don't get so high and mighty that no one can tell you anything because that is when you open the door for Satan to capture you by your ignorance.

123 Everything you need to do what God has called you to do is inside of you. All you need to do is find it and learn how to use it for God. He will reveal all things to you as you spend time in His presence.

124 God said "come as you are" but don't allow the enemy to make you believe it is okay to stay that way. God wants to see you mature in Christ.

125 Stop talking about everything that everyone else needs to do and focus on what God has called you to do. Maybe your movement will make someone else make a change.

126 Don't keep asking God to fix what is broken because He has something new and better for you if you will just let go of the old.

127 A simple act of kindness can change someone's life. It's not always about what someone can do for you but what you can do for someone else that will change your life.

128 There's no one like our Father. His mercy and grace keeps you through love.

129 Everything you go through is so someone else can make it through on your testimony. So keep pressing and know that you're not doing this in vain. Christ did it and so can you.

130 Like a child we must find joy in the smallest things, we must believe in the biggest things, and we must see God's goodness in all things because it's all good.

131 Many people will stick around when you're doing great things but only the ones sent by God will stay to endure with you.

132 You keep waiting on a fortune to come in but until you totally submit to God's will you will always live with barely enough because it's not about you but building His kingdom.

133 When God has a place for you to be Satan will do EVERYTHING to stop you but NOTHING will hinder God's move in your life except you.

134 God doesn't worry about His wellbeing because He is God and you shouldn't stress over yours if you know the God you serve. He will take care of you if you trust Him. Relax

135 It's your time to get up and move. You have been waiting for God to open doors but if you just sit around waiting there is no faith with works so what does God work with?

136 Shine today with the love God has put in you. Share that love with someone who is in need today. What good is it to have the love of God if you keep it to yourself?

137 You must continue to confess what the Lord has said so that you remember no situation can overpower God's promise to you.

138 Everything you have was provided by the Lord so you have no right to be stingy; you are blessed to be a blessing.

139 There is no better place to be than in the hands of God. He can fight your battles and shift things in your life while continuing to hold you up and protect you.

140 No matter what it seems like God has a plan for you so if you don't understand why you're going through what you are just know you're **GOING THROUGH** and it's not meant for you to stay there.

141 There's a faith struggle and Satan is going to attack you wherever you're weak: finances, sex, love, alcohol, ECT. but you have to trust God and let Him heal you through truth so you will be free.

142 You ask God to help you be you are not willing to help yourself because you don't want to let go of those things that hurt you.

143 When God gives you a word He will bring it to pass, it may not be in your time but it will happen because He is faithful as long as you are faithful to Him.

144 Why is it easy for you to trust in other people before you trust in God? Isn't God capable of doing more than any person because He created all? Where is your trust?

145 The storm is behind you and the sun is shining ahead, you just have to ignore what you hear behind you, because that's your past, and stay in God's hands.

146 In the morning meet with God and ask that His will be done, that He would protect you from you because sometimes you hurt yourself by your own words not the enemy.

147 To hell with what the devil has to say! Victory is in the hand of the Beholder and you are in God's hands so you are VICTORIOUS!

148 You can't wait for God to bless you before you can bless someone else because God sees your heart through your acts of sacrifice and He will acknowledge them and reward you.

149 Peace, be still. Know that God has got everything under control. Don't allow the thoughts that the enemy puts in your head to consume you. Just believe God.

150 God spoke the world into existence so how much more can He do for you just by speaking a word. You have the same power in you so you can form your world by the words you speak.

151 Where is your faith? If you are focusing on the problem you can't see the solution, which is Jesus.

152 God wants to bless you, not for you for someone else but you're going to go through some pain, not for you but for someone else. When you focus on your pain you miss God's plan.

153 Be careful how you talk to people because what you think is nothing may destroy a person. Be wise to speak from the spirit and not your flesh because God will see and judge you accordingly.

154 Follow God closely, and make sure you hear Him clearly so that you don't make the mistake of trusting false saints. A lot of people seem to mean well but are not sent from God so listen to Him.

155 You are not always going to like what God has for you to do but it's not about you. It's about God getting the glory.

156 Lord, let me walk in Your way, let me think like You, let me speak like You, let me model You.

157 Don't wait for other people to make time for you in their lives because you are so valuable to God that He always has time for you and that is all that matters.

158 You feel that you have to prove things to other people because you are dealing with insecurities that God needs to deliver you from. Now that you know you just need to ask for deliverance.

159 Jesus didn't force you into salvation so you don't have a right to push it on others but don't sit in the midst of those that are sinning if your spirit is telling you to get up and go.

160 Yes, you have been through some things but you have to know that all things happen for a reason and God will restore you if you believe so that you can be a testimony for Him.

161 Why would God withhold any good thing from you? If He is saying "no" or "wait" then trust that He has a reason and if you listen He will cover you from the plot of the enemy.

162 The things you refuse to do God will find someone else to do but no one can fulfill your purpose but you . . . there is someone that is hurt that only you can help.

163 If you would humble yourself and come to God, not with your own agenda, but seeking Him, He would willingly provide whatever you need.

164 You have to die to all your old ways so that you will arise in the new creation that God has called you to be.

165 Draw close to Jesus, like children, and be attentive to His every word.

166 You can quote the scriptures all day but it is NOT until you UNDERSTAND its true meaning that it can be applied to your life.

167 Don't treat Jesus like a credit card, leaving Him in your back pocket until you need Him and only giving Him your minimum, when He gave and still gives you His all.

168 When you become passionate about someone or something you will commit your whole being to it and it won't matter what anyone else says about it. What are you committed to?

169 If you are looking for security in a person it will never fill the void that you have because only God can give you true security and make you whole.

170 Don't wait until you get your life right before you come to God because you'll never do it on your own. Come as you are and He will make you the righteousness you are trying to reach.

171 Temptation is a part of flesh so you will always battle with it but you just need to trust in God to see you through. Even Jesus was tempted but rejoice because He overcame the world and so can you.

172 When you become saved, the Righteousness of God, there should be some things that you just don't do anymore . . . you won't change everything over night but you won't have any attraction to certain things anymore.

173 God is a giver but you have to learn to be a receiver. He cannot force you to take your blessings . . . you have to open up to receive them.

174 God is seeking to reach the stressed, depressed, and all who are stuck in a mess. You will come out of this and the sun will shine on you when you find Him and forsake everything else.

175 It's tragic to think of how bad people treat each other, even Christians, but you must know that they are speaking out of pain and at those times they need your love and prayers more than ever.

176 It is time to get into that quiet place so that you can clearly hear the voice of God.

177 The same God that gave it to you once can give it to you again if you believe.

178 No one can change the way that God feels about you. You are His child, the apple of His eye, He sent His only begotten Son to die so that you could be with Him forever. Don't let anyone tell you that you are not worthy of love.

179 Everything isn't always going to be fair but you have to continue to lift up your hands because in every little act of faith God strengthens you to go on.

180 Your destiny is predestined by God, not chosen by you, but it is up to you to choose to accept it or turn away. However there is no reward in going your own way when God always knows what's right.

181 It's very hard to accept you have made a mistake when you are trying so hard to live right because the enemy is going to boast on your slip until you want to give up but lift your eyes because your Father still loves you.

182 It doesn't matter what anyone says or what a situation looks like when you know what God has promised you. This is just the battleground but you already know the outcome . . . YOU WIN!

183 Sometimes it seems hard to give to someone else when you feel you are barely surviving as it is but God is faithful to take care of you when you help others in need.

184 I have been tested and I have come out as gold but only I can share my testimony and if I never tell a soul all that I went through was in vain.

185 God has not forgotten your tears and He is your vengeance but you must forgive those who have hurt you because you are standing in the way of your own freedom.

186 Don't be fooled to believe that going to church while you are living in sin will get you into Heaven. God knows your heart, and there is a difference between falling but getting back up and just staying down.

187 There is no beauty greater than the beauty of the Spirit. Even the most attractive people (outwardly) cannot compete with a humbled servant of God because beauty shows in everything they do.

188 You can never excel in what God has called you to do if you refuse to be taught. Without knowledge how will you know what is of God and what isn't?

189 If you speak life the enemy and his traps will be blocked but you must first think life because out of the abundance of the heart the mouth speaks.

190 Satan always wants you to look at your history, at the many things that haven't gone right, all the pain that you have had but if you look deeper in to history, at the story of Jesus, you will see His suffering and rejoice in what He has done for you. Forget about your history because His story is the only one that matters.

191 Rejoice in the Lord because He has given you victory but you have to choose to walk in it. No matter what you may be facing God has already defeated it so declare victory.

192 As a human it is by habit that you sin but God is forgiving if you repent. It doesn't matter what anyone else says about you . . . stand unashamed because God has called you righteous.

193 You can always see the faults in others when you can't see them in yourself. It's not up to you to check them . . . your focus should be on checking yourself and leaving the rest to God.

194 It takes patience to understand and accept the will of God for you. He will reveal it to you in His own time and it may not be what you want but it will be what's best.

195 It is morning and yesterday is over so put your all into what God has for you today because your past was to be learned from to teach someone else today.

196 God has given you the key to your breakthrough through His word . . . its up to you to use it. You are not a baby anymore so you must take charge and stop looking to be rescued.

197 You go through many struggles in life, and if you let them they will break you, but it was never meant for you to fix yourself . . . give it to God.

198 I love you. That's not just something to say but those words are true. God has placed you in my life for a reason & I hope you get what you need from me, as I will you.

199 You should never run from what God has ordained you to do, but run toward it because your true blessing is found in the work He created you to do.

200 You serve the only real God & He requires that you be real too. He loves you enough to correct you in your fakeness by taken off your mask & revealing who you really are.

201 Jesus is the reason for every season! Thank God for salvation.

202 The best 3 things, the only things that matter: God loves you, I love you & no matter what love conquers all. Love cannot be purchased, it's a gift.

203 God's kindness & love brings about His mercy in your time of weakness but you can't get comfortable in staying in your weakness because He wants to make you strong.

204 Today is the start of a new beginning. God's blessings fall, love holds, peace comforts, joy fills, truth makes wise & I am restored, refreshed, renewed!

205 In searching for God you find that it's in the little things that you feel Him the most. To truly love God you have to have a heart for His people—no substitute will do.

206 People awe at the beautiful house, wishing they were blessed to have it but they can't know what's inside-whether empty, or full of sin. Be thankful not envious.

207 Everyday you wake you should thank God for salvation. It's good to have health & wealth but only being saved, through the blood of Jesus, will matter in the end.

208 It is ONLY when your love for God out scales your desires & struggles that your test will become our testimony.

209 We struggle much with God being Ruler of our lives but in making the decision to surrender ALL to God we will find a place of peace even in the storms.

210 Praise God for the joy of the Lord because it overflows. I pray for you to have the peace that passes all understanding & overwhelming joy always.

211 If you don't worship Him (not only will the rocks cry out, but) you will worship something (self, work, relationships, ECT) because you were created to worship.

212 God says, "I have loved you from the beginning & I will never stop. I will never leave you but I will continue to draw you to Me & put others around that 2 love Me."

213 You have a calling & it is time you submit WILLINGLY because it's not about you but the ones God wants to claim for the Kingdom so step into His purpose for you.

214 God is great for He has given you another day to get it right. You should be so humbled in knowing you don't deserve any of His grace so be wise to do well today.

215 You focus so much time on what you are not doing with your life then spend even more time thinking about what you should be doing that you never start DOING!

216 Jesus, where would I be if You had not saved me? If You took Your grace away I would not be here today. I will sing praises to Your name for everyday You are the same!

217 Eyes do not see, ears do not hear, the mysteries of God—only in the Spirit will you find the truth that sets free—all questions lead to one—God knows all!

218 God has promised you peace in the storm. Why not take hold? In the fullness of joy you can dance in the rain no matter how hard it may fall.

219 Through Christ you ALREADY have the victory now you just have to bring it into the physical so keep fighting because it ain't over until God says it's over!

220 The greatest love was shown through Christ sacrifice. If you are to be like Him you must be self-sacrificing in love to one another. Don't just say it. 1 John 3:16-23

221 You declare things in the spirit but don't experience them because you doubt and walk in disobedience. You're hindering yourself while God is waiting on you to get right.

222 In spite of me God's will has to be done. It's not me; it's Him who needs to be pleased.

223 It's a war for your life and the devil doesn't play fair. He will do ANYTHING to kill you and keep you from fulfilling God's purpose in your life.

224 God says, "There are so many things I want to take from you. Things from your past that have held you victim but I need you to let go. It wasn't your fault so release it to Me."

225 The things you go through are to make you stronger but not to build brick walls around your heart. Satan has thrown a lot of things at you that have made it hard but God wants to give you a new heart. His heart. You just have to receive it.

226 Why do you attempt to do it all yourself? You were not worthy to shed your own blood at the cross but love saved you. Your only requirement is to take Him in daily.

227 You weren't born righteous BUT thank God when you received Christ as Lord you were born again into righteousness.

228 Yes, I'm pressing towards that goal . . . I have what God promised me. I have sown and NOW is my time for my harvest to produce IN JESUS NAME!

229 You say, "Speak Lord, we need a word from You. I won't move until You speak . . . speak, speak, speak!" When will you close your mouth to listen? Be still and know . . .

230 Don't be rushed going to and fro . . . be patient, walk slow, turn off your mind . . . so you can hear God speaking.

231 Will when your will line up with His? If you decide to walk in your own way to abide in your own will, you defeat the purpose of saying that God reigns over you.

232 God is your portion. He is not going to sow everything for you while you reap all the benefits. If you choose to sow nothing you choose to reap the same.

233 Everything you want has already been provided now God is waiting on you so your blessings will be released. You know what He wants . . . what are you waiting for?

234 Through God ALL things are possible! He has made me glad in my soul and I will ALWAYS rejoice because His goodness has covered me through ALL things!

235 God says, "Come in to Me. Press in to My presence. NO MATTER WHAT press through to My heart with your praise. I AM your healing, your deliverance, I AM your BREAKTHROUGH." Selah

236 Some think being high is an incredible feeling but that is only a temporary fix. A supernatural high is to be overflowing with God's spirit. GET A GOD HIGH!

237 Close your eyes—see that ministry, house, car, family-that's where God wants you to be. Open your eyes—this is the process that's going to get you there.

238 Your prayers are only effective when YOU believe what you are speaking. If you are doubting it's possible than you don't believe God can do all.

239 Praise Him in advance for the blessing and be obedient to allow the Holy Spirit to move in your vessel.

240 Rejoice! God has given you new mercy. Everything you did or didn't do is in the past, forgive YOURSELF, stat the day fresh, and glorify Him in ALL that you do.

241 To anticipate Gods move in your life you have to line up with His will for your life. Expecting Gods blessings without total commitment is wasted energy.

242 In this race you are going to be tired and feel pain. Some times you'll have to push through the hurt and other times you'll have to let God carry you and just rest in Him.

243 Lord, fill my heart with worship for You and overwhelm me with Your joy and peace. Refresh my spirit and mind as I seek You. In Jesus' name Amen

244 Complete submission! Don't just love God—fall in love with Him. It is the best feeling to be in love and you always say yes to the one who has your heart.

245 No matter how much you cry or how loud you scream no one will know the depth of your pain but **GOD** that is why He is your comfort so you can give those things to Him.

246 Thank God for that hunger and thirst . . . that longing to be full because it's for Him. Now redirect it to the right source so He can fill that void.

247 BREATHE! Release those things and people of yesterday. If you become content with holding your past like a security blanket God can't give you anything new.

248 Stop allowing satan to tell you that you can't win. You have all the strength you need and when it seems like a struggle just praise God and He will bring you through.

249 Allow God to free you from that heavy heart. There is no need to kill yourself trying to carry a burden that Christ already died for.

250 I pray God fills you with His peace and joy. Smile, laugh, love, say hi to everyone you meet and let your light so shine . . . Matthew 5:16!

251 True love is a battle. Jesus made the ultimate sacrifice. God has equipped you with the Holy Spirit so you may fight the good fight to be with Him forever!

252 Thank God for who He is, was, and will always be forever. No matter what you go through He will never change because you do. He is holy and no one can compare!

253
1. Song in my heart
2. Peace in my soul
3. Radiance of God flowing out my body
   I'm ready to start my day!

254 Don't second guess the blessings that God has promised you. Although if may seem impossible or as if it will never happen but keep your hope in God and He'll do it.

255 If you use your whole heart God will bless it from the start.

256 Satan is going to always attack you where he knows God is still working on you at so you just have to close your mouth, guard your heart, and press through praising God.

257 YOUR BODY is the church of the living God. When you praise you BLESS GOD in your temple. IT'S TIME TO GO TO CHURCH RIGHT NOW!!!

258 There is a void that needs to be filled. There is a search that seems to be never-ending. When will you stop looking and just ask the God who knows all?

259 The reason you fight God on what He is doing is because you can't see His perfect plan. Stop worrying and just know He IS and He KNOWS when you don't.

260 SHUT UP! So many times you open your mouth to say things that bring mess you don't need in your life. Why won't you open your mouth and speak life?

261 BE THANKFUL you are in this place because you need to be. EVERYTHING you need to make it through is right in front of you. TRUST you are coming out as pure gold.

262 Silence all that is around you and make God your center of attention. Let Him hold you and breathe His love and peace into you.

263 Don't allow satan to keep throwing your past back in your face. God loves you in spite of who you were. Shut the devil up by being the person God sees you as.

264 God is calling you to move forward. He wants to give you so much more but He has to prepare you first to receive. Let go, let God and move to the next level.

265 When you feel stuck, distant, or alone just begin to call on Jesus and He will answer you. Even when it feels like nothing has changed He is working it out.

266 Worship the Sovereign God, Ruler of your heart. The love He has for you cannot be measured or reached but you can love Him with everything that is in you.

267 As much as you expect from God, He expects from you.

268 Take the wings God has given you and lift yourself up to a place of excellence.

269 You may think you are going the wrong way but you aren't . . . yet it's good to be watchful. Other times you know you are going wrong but you are content to not hear God . . . hmm

270 You have to find a way to push through the pain into praise because your hurt won't become healing if you refuse to let it go.

271 We were all given gifts from God to use for the glory of God. It's up to you if you use them to glorify God or if you let them go to waste to glory in the world.

272 Jesus said, "let nothing offend you" so no matter what someone says or does don't let it offend you because you are to love them with the love of God in spite of themselves.

273 Don't speak what you see because you will continue to walk in that direction . . . speak what you know **GOD IS ABLE** to do in your life so that you may be turned in another direction.

274 God says, "Focus your hearts' desires on Me. You are My child and I will take care of you if you trust in Me so don't worry about tomorrow just have peace in today."

275 The core of who you are rises up in how you treat others and conduct yourself. It's not about what your say but what you do that shows if you have Christ heart.

276 There is nothing you can do that will take away the Fathers love or that you can't be forgiven for so don't let guilt keep you from being with Him because He hasn't left you.

277 Don't look at what everyone else is doing or what they have, just keep your eyes focused on your goal so that you don't miss your target.

278 Make sure your heart is lined up with the will of God so when you reap what you sow it will be of a good harvest, pleasing to God and not just yourself.

279 If you take the time to appreciate what you already have in life God will see your gratitude and bless you with more.

280 Sometimes it's hard to see past the present state. Sometimes all there is left to do is pray for wisdom and understanding to find your way out.

281 Sometimes you don't get what you want because God is protecting you from the pain you don't see that comes from the desire you so desperately want.

282 Being in the world you get caught up with the ways of the world, worrying about not having, but as God's child you know you are taken care of so trust that He is true.

283 Letting go of pain hurts but it will only hurt you more if you continue to hold on to it. Trials come your way to make you stronger not to break you so give it to God.

284 You are the one that God has put here to touch that person . . . so if you never speak how will they know you were spent by God to change their life?

285 When God speaks it is up to you to listen and act. Sometimes you can stand at a door that will never lead you to where you want to go while you miss the doors He has opened.

286 The joy of being a mother or father can't be replaced, whether you have biological, step, adopted or spiritual children or just helped raise your siblings. You impacted a life.

287 We all have struggles but you can't go through them alone that is why God places you in a church family so you can lean on each other when you can't stand alone.

288 You need to know the difference between faith and foolishness. Every word is not God's word and only faith is backed by the word. The only way not to be caught in foolishness is to study the Word.

289 Everything that comes your way is not your blessing, sometimes it's sent to block your real blessing so you must seek wisdom so you won't open a door that's not for you.

290 God has put a seed in you that is going to reap a great harvest but it's in His time. A farmer knows that he can't continue to dig the seed up and expect a change.

291 You have to be faithful to walk this walk . . . when times get hard you can't look for the first exit but you have to trust that God will see you through because His word is true.

292 Jesus said "follow me" then He was beat and hung on the cross for your freedom. He didn't say the walk wouldn't be hard or painful but that it would be worth it.

293 Sometimes you want God to speak to you when He only wants to touch because there are times when only a touch from the Father will suffice.

294 You never know what someone is going through in their heart but God put you in their life because they need you so meet that need and when you're in need someone will meet yours.

295 Sometimes life doesn't go as you plan but all things happen for a reason. Only God knows what that is so you must trust Him that your pain is not in vain.

296 You never know what tomorrow holds but you know what yesterday took away so hold to God's hand and make the most of today.

297 God will change nothing in the world until something is changed in the church . . . the church won't change until something is changed in you. Let Him alter your heart.

298 It's amazing that you can forward messages, help others and give offerings hoping to receive a blessing but when God says, "do nothing, just trust Me and wait" you can't.

299 You have been hurt by where you are right now and thinking about where you were but it's time to renew your mind knowing this to shall pass for the Lord will see you through.

300 Things may look hard right now and you may feel like it's not getting any better but know that you will win if you can endure so keep your head up and say AMEN.

301 God never said to lay down and let people walk on you but He did say you must be a servant before you can become a leader so serve one another and Christ did.

302 You can say that you believe as much as you want but until you stop believing with your head and start believing with your heart you won't get anywhere.

303 When you feel like giving up, GIVE UP A SACRIFICE. If you make a true sacrifice then God will show up to prove that He is God.

304 When you are about to be blessed chaos seems to break out in your life but know when you have no control that God is in control.

305 There is no obstacle that is too big for God but it is according to your faith . . . do you believe your Big God can wipe out your little obstacle?

306 Retreat to look at where you are so you can plan where you're going because God didn't intend on you staying in one place so sometimes you have to take a step back to move forward.

307 Jesus paid for freedom but you are still bound . . . not because of what you don't know but what you don't believe . . . God can't change your life if you won't change your mind (faith).

308 God has given everyone a destiny to fulfill but most will never reach it because they waste time on chasing empty dreams instead of asking God to reveal His purpose for them.

309 It's good to have peace in the middle of a storm . . . understand that you control your mind storms so if God isn't moved by it then why are you?

310 God didn't intend on your relationship with Him being a religious act practiced a few times a week but He wants intimacy and realness that comes from really knowing Him.

311 There's an emptiness that only God can fill . . . the problem is you tell God how you want Him to fill it and with what instead of letting Him be God . . . who knows best?

312 It's hard to do right when you allow your flesh to control you. Press through what you have always done so you can do what you know you should.

313 If you are honored to serve God you should be humbled to serve each other no matter the task because it is for the King and whatever you do to the least you do unto Him.

314 Responsibility is a choice. Jesus chose to be responsible for your sins so that you could be free. Now your responsibility is to let His light shine through you.

315 It is your responsibility to help others as God makes you able, even if it's just spending time with them, because God called you to lift one another up when they are down.

316 You don't ask certain people or circumstances to be in your life but it will make you wiser and stronger . . . if you let it. God will work it out for your good and His glory.

317 Just remember not to look at the situation but at the God you serve and He will put everything together. The struggle is to make you stronger but you have to stay in the word and lean on God so He will move.

318 Your destiny is predestined by your trials so you may have suffered but the pain cannot compare to the blessing that is coming if you can endure a little longer.

319 God is a RESTORER of all things (joy, peace, love, finances, health, life) but you have to believe that He can do all and praise Him for who He is. So look up.

320 You are not meant to sit down on your beliefs but to rise up in God's boldness. No longer will obstacles or people trample on you but you will rise and speak the WORD!

321 Your most important accomplishments could never be done without God enabling you so it is just as important to invite Him into everything that is important to you.

322 Put your trust in God so that you may be able to trust yourself and to be able to trust others around you because God has put us here together because we need each other.

323 Pray and ask God what He wants you to do. If He has promised you something He will do what He said but situations always come to stop you from getting where God wants you to go . . . it's up to you if you allow it to stop you from getting your blessing.

324 Hindrances come but NOTHING BUT YOU can stop you from fulfilling the destiny God has planned for you. Don't let your mind talk you out of receiving your promises.

325 Some things can't be explained, like the sun, moon and stars but you answer its just God so when you don't know why He loves you despite your issues . . . HE IS JUST GOD.

326 Stop trying to be perfect but let a perfect God deal with your imperfections. Stop looking at others to count your faults and just be you. Don't try to act holy just be holy.

327 Morning has come and it is time to rise. God is renewing your strength and joy so rise up into your destiny because the night is over and morning has come.

328 God's presence is in this place but it's up to you to tap in to His power. I pray that you allow the Holy Spirit to consume you and raise you up to a new level.

329 God is calling you to EXACT OBEDIENCE. By no means will He continue to except your halfhearted praise and compromises on His word. It's all or nothing at all.

330 It is important to keep your hands lifted to God. Even though your arms may get tired and start to hurt push through . . . if you drop your arms how will you catch your blessing?

331 Worship is not JUST music but a lifestyle. It's how you live your life to honor God and show how much you TRULY love Him. Is your worship pleasing to Him?

322 If you don't expect God to move in greater ways than you can imagine than you'll miss it. So expect Great things NOW. I RECEIVE IT IN JESUS NAME SO BE IT!

333 God says, "You don't have to rush, for if I set the date I will bring everything together at the appointed time. Just take the steps that I say and enjoy the walk."

334 God has given us the victory although sometimes all we can see is defeat but don't allow your feelings to be hurt by the situation keep your eyes on God and ALLOW Him to bring you through.

335 Thank You, Lord, for being in the midst of every situation. I KNOW Jehovah is greater than ALL and no matter what it looks like You have already caused me to triumph.

336 Your love can never amount to the love God has for you but you should always do our best to love others as Christ does by seeing the God in them.

337 God doesn't do half-baked blessings. When He says He is going to bless you it won't be any burdens on you. God is complete in all that He does and always on time.

338 If you always believe God for only the little things then you'll never come out of your comfort zone BUT the same God's blessings are never little.

339 Give God praise despite what everyone else thinks about you because people will ALWAYS have something to say so what. Be crazy and give God the glory because only He matters.

340 It's not for you to always understand God's plan because His works are mysterious but He wants you to willingly submit because He knows what's best and wants you to have it even MORE.

341 I seek Your face to understand the wisdom of You, all Your mysteries. Show me Your face, I pray, so that I can really know You. In Jesus name AMEN!

342 God has given you gifts but you have to go to Him in order to know how to use them so that the Kingdom may be built because your gifts are not for you but for others.

343 SMILE. It may FEEL like God isn't hearing any of your prayers and you think you have to work things out on your own BUT when you are at your lowest point God is MOST HIGH . . .

344 Your focus should not be on what others think or say but what God says and not to allow anything to pollute the anointing God has given you to do His work. Selah

345 All that you search for is in God but too many times you don't want to turn to Him because you are afraid of committing to Him. Don't miss your blessing because you're afraid.

346 Don't make God your last option when everything else fails you because He promised never to leave or forsake you from the beginning and He has the answer you need.

347 It's easy to be deceived when something looks righteous but ask God to open your eyes to all situations so that you will see what's real and what's fake.

348 You can pray as much as you want but if you don't truly believe it profits you nothing. You must know before you pray that it's already done and thank God in advance.

349 When God delivers you it is so you will NOT be bound anymore but what good is it to you if you continue to live the same way. Freedom and captivity is your choice.

350 God is your source of all things if you trust in Him. There is nothing you can think that He doesn't know. Surely mercy and goodness will follow you for a lifetime . . .

351 God speaks ALL the time but He needs a vessel to speak through and you should accept the call because through your love for Him.

352 When the morning comes everything is better but you just have to make it through the night. It may be dark but hold to your promise because morning is a brighter day.

353 I pray you no longer complain about your pain but go through rejoicing and know that your pain will be used to heal others and give them hope. IN JESUS NAME AMEN.

354 You work so hard to hold on to your blessings but don't fail to realize that you are blessed to be a blessing and as you pour out God will bless you with something better.

355 This is a test of the times: when everything around you seems to be falling apart will you still know that God is working it out for you?

356 You praise God when you receive a blessing but forget to praise Him just for your everyday blessings. Everyday gives you a reason to stay in continual praise.

357 It's time to go to a new level in Christ but first you have to stop being afraid of what you don't know and just dive into what God has for you. Stop searching and just go . . .

358 There is a fire that burns in you to do God's will but life's challenges come to blow the flame out. Go to the Father to have your fire renewed . . . your going to make it.

359 Some times the fear doesn't leave but that is why God has given His Spirit so that we push through with God's strength to conquer the impossible.

360 Don't be afraid of what you see because this won't last always. Lift your head and smile . . . the harder the struggle seems the greater the blessing and breakthrough IS!

361 What is this deep love God has for us? He loves you even when you are in mess and pulls at your heart to get it right. A love that makes you want to be right so DO IT!

362 There is a place you can go when it seems you are beat. Where God can restore what life has stolen but it will cost you a sacrifice of praise. Can you afford it?

363 A lot of things may seem like God's favor but the enemy will send an anti-blessing before your real blessing comes so pray for God's will before you accept just anything.

364 Don't allow people around you to cause you to think that you are missing something by living for God. He made you to be different and because you choose to walk with Him you will be blessed with more than anything the world could try to withhold from you. What God promises is greater than what the world denies.

365 God is always guiding you if you would just look up and stop walking in circles with your head down. You will never get out of where you are if you don't look up to the hills.

366 Consider where you are and where God has brought you from . . . know that He has so much more in store for you if you would only submit to Him.